Stories of a Street Performer

Copyright© 2012 by Whit Haydn & ....
ISBN-13: 978-1-937981-29-7
Author: Whit "Pop" Haydn
Editor: Kambiz Mostofizadeh
Publisher: Mikazuki Publishing House

www.MikazukiPublishingHouse.com

STREET MAGIC

The streets and market places of the city are an ancient venue for magic. At least since Greek and Roman times, magicians and sleight-of-hand performers have entertained and distracted those who came from far places to buy and sell in the public square. Athenæus, in his *Deipnosophistæ*, describes a cups and balls performer at a Greek theatre:

A certain man stepped into the midst, and placed on a three-legged table three small cups, under which he concealed some little white round pebbles such as are found on the banks of rivers; these he placed one by one under the cups, and then, I don't know how, made them appear under another cup and finally showed them in his mouth.[1]

In first century Rome, Seneca enjoyed the mystery of these sleight-of-hand tricks seen in the street: "If I get to know how a trick is done, I lose my interest in it." [2]

Down through the centuries, the street magician has

fascinated and amused the throng, and has been a part of the fun and adventure of journeying to the square. More than this, the street performer offers the most honest of entertainments. The public is invited to watch and enjoy. The children and the poor get a show for free. Those with money pay what they think the show was worth—and not until after they have seen the performance. No one has to stick around if the show lags; no one has to endure a lackluster performance. The conditions under which the street performer must ply his craft are stringent. He is usually, though not always, surrounded. He must call and hold a crowd for the length of the performance. He must deal with hecklers, distractions, weather, and sometimes keep an eye out for the authorities. He has to keep a constant watch on his tip basket and his props, or these will likely wander off into the crowd.

He must keep the crowd interested and amused, but he must also be able to convert Their attention into excitement and energy. He must then convert this into enthusiasm for his cause to have the spectators shower him with money.

The street performer gets an education in the nitty-gritty of show business that is unlike anything that can be obtained elsewhere. In the old vaudeville days, performers would work many shows a day, and travel, live, and work with the other acts. The dancers would learn a little juggling, the magician would learn the comic's routines, skills and information were traded, and acts were polished and honed. The ability to perform in front of an audience many times a day, as in the dime museums, circus, carnivals, burlesque, Chautauqua and vaudeville circuits is not common today. The street is one of the places where a performer can learn his craft by performing it.

I was lucky enough to get my start in magic as a street performer back in the 1960's. That was in many ways, a truly wonderful time for performers in alternative entertainment. It was a revival of sorts, and there were very few of us. It was new and interesting for the audiences. The Sixties was a time of ferment and excitement. I lived in the East Village of Manhattan in 1969-70, and worked in the West Village usually in the 6th Ave/8th Street area, as well as in Washington Square Park. In 1974, I worked my way around England, Scotland, and Wales, and spent time in Paris, where I worked the Left Bank. I performed standard magic for tips on the street and in parks, as well as busking around in bars, something I did mainly when the weather was cold. I also performed the shell game and three-card monte on occasion, but not in a mob game. It was one on one, for very little money, something I did mainly for my own education. Nobody was ever taken for a whole lot, but mainly because without shills this is difficult, and I didn't know anything about using shills. Nevertheless, I frequently made more than I could by passing the hat after a magic show. At that time the police were not aware of, and had no interest in these swindles. No one had done them on the streets in New York City for years. And with the anti-war protests, Black Panther demonstrations, Weathermen bombings, drugs, violent crime and other concerns— the police probably just didn't think it was worth the bother. I sometimes even had cops come up and watch the game for a while and then walk on. By the mid seventies, the game had become a nuisance all over town.

I had an ESP act that I would work around the tables in a bar when the weather was bad. This included my impromptu card code that later became *A*

Routine for the Blind. When the police were not letting me stop pedestrian traffic, I also used a mind-reading scam I call the *ESP Survey* that I did one-on-one in the street using a nail-writer. Both of these will be described later.

I continued working in around Dupont Circle in Washington, D.C. through 1974, at which point I joined a traveling improvisational political theater troupe called the **Road Company**, directed by Bob Leonard. I did unicycle, fire eating, magic and juggling for the performances, as well as acting in the improvisational plays. From there I began performing in amusement parks and other venues as a magician, and have not worked the streets since that time. Many of my favorite routines, including the *Comedy Four Ring Routine* and *The Mongolian Pop-Knot*, and almost all of my performing attitudes developed during the period when I worked on the streets. But this is not a "how to" treatise on street performing. Instead, we will discuss some of the important things that any performer can learn from studying the methods and attitudes of the street. There have been many good books written on street performing recently. These have much better information on the permits, conditions and venues available, and on how to go about making a living performing on the street today, than I could present. I have been away from the street venue for so many years, that many things have change, much of the advice I could give on how to go about it would be dated. But certain general principles can be learned from street performing that will apply to other performing situations.

Street Stories

My street performing began because of my bad eyesight. I had been studying magic since I was ten, and had the good fortune to be helped along by two wonderful North Carolina magicians, Dick Snavely and Bill Tadlock. Both of them were big influences on me. Through them I met Wallace Lee of Durham, who also had quite an impact on my thinking as I started out. Most of my orientation was toward stage magic, but I loved all of it. When I was fourteen, I even persuaded my parents to let me take a Greyhound bus trip alone across country to attend Abbott's Get-Together. It was my first magic convention. My interest in magic continued through high school, but I neglected the study of magic during the turbulent days of the Sixties on a college campus. During my college days at East Carolina University, I had been heavily involved in both the civil rights and anti-war movements. I worked with the Southern Christian Leadership Conference, as an aide to Golden Frinks, the state field secretary of the SCLC. I was beaten up and arrested in my work with voter registration drives.

I became involved with the anti-war movement on campus, and eventually in 1969 I left college to challenge the draft. I was one of the first persons to receive conscientious objector status from Pitt County, North Carolina, and was assigned to New York University Hospital to do my alternative service. After arriving in New York, I found a railroad flat in an apartment building on the lower East Side. The ancient elevator in the building always smelled of urine. My kitchen had a claw-foot iron bathtub next to the stove. A linoleum counter fit over the top of it, and served as a kitchen counter. To take a bath, you had to put the cover on the floor. The apartment door was fitted with three deadbolts and a police lock that was a bar that fastened in a plate on the floor that could be locked against the door with a bolt. The apartment building was on East 1st Street and 2nd Avenue and my apartment went for $76 dollars a month (I can't but wonder what it goes for now), and was located just a half block from the Catholic Worker. This was a pacifist group that I had some connections with through a radical priest, Father Charlie Mulholland, whom I had worked with in North Carolina. The Catholic Worker produces a well-known newspaper and runs a soup kitchen for the homeless. Dorothy Day was the founder, and she was one impressive lady, one of the most dedicated people I have ever met. The people at the Worker helped me to get established in the East Village where I worked as a volunteer military counselor. They also helped me find a roommate, another young guy who came from the Midwest. I began work at NYU Hospital in inhalation therapy.

When the army called me for my physical, I failed because of my eyesight, as I am terribly near-sighted. Suddenly I was out of the draft and into the cold. I eventually lost my job at the hospital which was held for those assigned to CO status. Without a paying job, I was sort of floundering. I remembered the street performers who were talked about in the magic history books, and had seen plenty of musicians playing for change on the streets. At the magic shop I heard about a guy named Jeff Sheridan who was doing magic for tips up in Central Park. So why couldn't a magician work the street? One evening I took a deck of cards, some rope, and my linking rings out to the West Village. I set up in front of a closed jewelry store on 8th Street, and began doing magic and passing the hat. I was astounded by the response! I made almost two hundred dollars in three hours. My roommate and I were convinced that this could really be a cool way to make a living. However, I had a much rougher time drawing a crowd the next few times I tried, and became a little more realistic. I had a lot more to learn about working a street act than I had realized.

Eventually, I found different strategies for drawing a crowd, holding their attention, and then getting them to pay me money. Various people helped me as I learned the craft. One of the most important of the early ones was the "Captain".

I was working on a street corner near the *Fillmore East* one night right after a show let out. I had a good crowd, and was doing okay. At the corner of the crowd was a man who looked about fifty-five with a few days growth of white beard. He was in a wheel chair, dressed in a pea coat and wore a skipper's hat. He seemed to enjoy the show and was laughing and commenting loudly to those around him how good I was. After the show, he wheeled over and said, "You're coming with me. We're going to make some money." I packed up and followed him to a nearby bar. He pulled his wheelchair up to the side of the door and then climbed down out of it. His legs were cut off just below the pelvis, and he moved by walking on his hands. He sauntered into the bar on his hands as if he owned the place, and then sat down, putting one hand on a bar stool, holding the other one out to me. "Give me a shoulder there, bud. Thanks." He lifted himself onto the stool and spun himself around a couple of times. Then he addressed everyone in the bar in an amazingly loud voice. There were maybe six people at the bar, and a couple of others playing pool. They all turned and stared at him. He cut quite an interesting figure. "Everyone come over here right now. Stop what you're doing and gather around. I have something really important for you to see. This bartender is about to buy me and my son here a drink. Because this kid is going to do something that will shake you up, and make you all laugh. He is a genius. Wait 'til you see what he can do with a deck of cards. This is the damnedest thing you ever saw. Come over here, honey. This lady wants to pick a card, don't you? You are going to choke when you see this. Show them your stuff, Junior." Before I knew it, I was performing everything I knew. The people ate it up. The bartender bought us each a drink. We stayed for over an hour. When the show was over, the "Captain" leaped into action again. He pulled off his cap and dropped off the barstool. He walked over to each person on his hands, sat down in front of them and held out the hat. "You can't tell me you see stuff like this everyday. Now come on. Give something to the cause. This boy was great, wasn't he? You laughed, didn't you? Now, show some appreciation here. I know you got more than that…" His manner was so authoritative and so demanding, and his stature so diminutive that people just laughed and dropped money into the hat. Most of them didn't look like they had much, but they put it in. When we left we had close to thirty dollars, which he split down the middle and then gave me half. He climbed into his wheelchair and as he started to wheel off, he said, "It's always hard to sell yourself. You and me make a good team. See ya' tomorrow."

I was performing in the same area for several days, but didn't see a sign of the "Captain". Eventually, he showed up again and spirited me off to several bars where we pulled the same stunt as before. He was truly awesome in the force of his will and his ability to get people to do what he wanted. I never found out his name. He always said, "Just call me "Captain". Over the next few weeks, I spent several days trying to keep up with that wheelchair. I began to believe that his story of having his gunrunning boat shot out from under him off the coast of Cuba might be true. That's how he said he lost his legs. But who knows? He always changed the subject when I asked him where he was from or other personal questions. He certainly had the manner of someone used to bossing others around. After one encounter at a bar where we made eighty dollars, he brought me over to his apartment in the ground floor of a really derelict-looking building. The apartment was filled with junk, but everything was very clean and ordered, shipshape. He made tea, and we talked. I don't remember much of what he said, but he did say one thing that stuck in my mind.

"Don't ask for stuff. You have to tell people what to do. Take over. Not in a bad way but in a friendly way. People want someone to direct. They are more comfortable when they know someone is in charge. When you are working, just say 'Take a card,' not 'Would you **please** take a card.' You are like the captain or the director. Just tell people what to do and they will do it. Take the situation over. Let people know what is expected of them. Let 'em know what you want. " I saw him a few more times, and then he just seemed to disappear. I could never forget the sheer force of his personality. And I think he was right about the attitude of the performer and the need for authority. The audience needs to be directed and told what you want from them. The performer is not the host and the audience his guests. The performer is the one running the show. You don't ask them to laugh, you make them laugh. I worked at the same spots quite a bit. You get to feel you own a spot, and then you are comfortable there. There might be better places, but it's good to feel you belong in a place. Everyone else is just visiting. It is very hard to drop your props somewhere and just begin working. It seems like you are breaking up what was going on by interrupting. I found that if I just stood in a place until I had been there longer than anyone else, I felt more like I owned it. People were coming through my space, and I had control. One such favorite spot was on 8th Street near 6th Avenue. There was a small jewelry store with display windows there, and it was closed at night. Anytime after six, I had a perfect little stage to work from, and the audience could gather around in a semi-circle on the sidewalk. The evening crowds in the West Village were good tippers, and had a relaxed attitude. They were going to music clubs and coffeehouses, not hurrying to a theater. I usually would draw fairly big crowds, but these blocked the sidewalks and brought attention from the police.

I started using a twelve-year old kid named Angel to watch for the police. He would stand at the back of the crowd and whistle if he saw a cop. I quickly began to rely on card tricks almost completely, because I could instantly stop the show, put the cards away, and spin around so that I was part of the crowd. When the cops arrived, there would be a whole crowd just staring in the shop window, and the cops would get visibly frustrated. The people in the audience thought it was hysterical, and it was kind of fun. It almost became a part of the act. Unfortunately, there was an Orange Julius shop just half a block away, and Angel loved Orange Julius. We had just divided the tip from the last crowd, and I had begun a new show. Without telling me, Angel went to get an orange drink. I had a card selected at one side of the crowd, and had just turned to the other side to have a second card selected when I saw a policeman standing at the front of the crowd. He was smiling with his thumbs stuck in his belt, and rocking back and forth on one foot. "Let's take a little walk," he said as the crowd booed. I put the cards away and followed him down the street to a coffee shop.

Another policeman was sitting at the counter having coffee. "Guess who I got here..." The second cop looked me over and said, "I don't know. Who?" The first cop said "This is the guy whose been blocking the sidewalk on 8th Street." "Oh, yeah. What's he selling?" "Nothin'. He does card tricks. Show my partner here a trick, kid." I spent fifteen minutes doing card tricks. I felt like the sheriff in the old west was making me dance to his 45 revolver. But they both seemed to like it. They each pulled out a dollar and gave it to me. The first officer said, "Don't let me catch you down there on 8th Street again. But there is a real good place just a few blocks away, we'll show you. It has the same kind of set up with the store window and pretty good traffic. You can work there and drive the guys in that precinct nuts for a while. If they catch you, tell them Jim and Eddie from over here sent you."

I sometimes would work at Washington Square Park, especially on pretty days on the weekend. Lots of people hung out there, mostly students and musicians. Sometimes I would perform silently with one of the bands, doing manipulative magic or juggling while they played. It helped draw tips because it gave people something to watch a show. Usually with the musicians, people would walk by and drop something in the instrument case, but they wouldn't draw a crowd, and they didn't get to work them for their money. By drawing attention to the group, and stopping every now and then to pass the hat, I was able to increase the take quite a bit. One of these musicians was a talented young black guy named Roland Henderson. He played

Indian music on sitar and tabla, and was extremely

good. We sometimes took a bus down to DC and

played in Dupont Circle for a change of scene.

Another musician I worked with was a jazz and pop

guitarist named Lester Fountain. He was in his forties

and made decent money performing in more

respectable venues, but he liked to spend his daytime

practicing outside while people dropped money on

him.

　　　These types of performances were a lot of fun

and a good way to pass a pretty day, but didn't

make a whole lot of money because it had to be split

so many ways. I was always very impressed by

the skill and devotion to their craft that these

musicians had. They were not usually very good at

making money.   Most of the time that I was in New

York I heard a lot about this great magician who

worked on the weekends in Central Park. His name

was Jeff Sheridan. I have since talked to him on the phone, but never got to see him work. He was a legend even then. At Tannen's I met an African-American magician who gave me a lot of good advice. Everett "Presto" Johnson was a man that I took to be in his forties. He showed me some of the fanciest sleight-of-hand I had ever seen; making four coins spin around each hand at the same time for example. He had been around, and knew a lot about performing in many different venues. He was very generous in his help. The best thing he taught me was to change my angle to fit the situation. For example, I liked to do some juggling and manipulation with billiard balls. Most of the time on the street, I couldn't do the billiard balls because of the bad angles with the shell. He told me to just change the angle. When I asked him what he meant, he said, "Well just go down on one knee and let the crowd look down at you. Play the shell to the ground. They will have to get below your hands to get an angle on you."

After that, I often performed with a small Bukhara carpet that I would unroll on the ground in a park. I could do the cups and balls on it, and go down on one knee to do billiard balls. People would stand all around in a circle and watch. It worked for the magic, but was not the best situation for making money. When people were crowded around like that, no one behind them could see. You could only work for the number of people in the immediate circle. To get a bigger crowd, you have to have height. The idea of changing the angle though, has stuck with me. I sometimes like to do the billiard balls or the Phoenix Aces at a private party or other situations in which I can't get my back to a wall. I go down on one knee and do it with the bad angle to the floor. I had a wand made that was very beautiful. It was almost an inch in diameter and about 14 inches long. It was solid walnut with the center section recessed and covered with a tooled leather sheath sewn with horse hair and covered with brass studs. Not only did it look like something that Merlin would have wielded, it was heavy enough to be of some protection in the sometimes dangerous world I was working in.

It is amazing how a young person can be so stupid. At that age, I thought I was immortal. I did many things that could have gotten me hurt, that even a few years later I wouldn't have thought of risking. For example, I used to spend the best part of the evening performing for the crowds in the West Village. I worked the streets during the crowded times, and then sometimes would end up performing later at what we called "basket houses." These were clubs like the one in the basement of the Olive Tree Café. Set up much like a comedy club today. At these clubs performers, mostly musicians and comedians, would work a set and then pass a basket around among the audience to collect tips. Some really great acts would work these places, as well as some truly abominable ones. The tourists were mostly gone at that point, so the audiences were often performers and bartenders or waitresses from other nightspots, all good tippers. After the show, I would often hang out with the musicians and other performers until the late hours. At that point I would have to walk home to the East Village, usually along 4th Street. This took me right through the worst part of the Bowery. And my pockets were usually bulging with coins and bills from the evening's work. At two o'clock in the morning, there was no telling whom you could meet up with down there. One night as I came past the 4th Street Mission, I saw another guy walking towards me on the other side of the street. He looked like just another longhaired, bearded dude, and we barely glanced at each other. But as we passed, I got a strange feeling that he looked familiar. When I turned to look at him, I realized that he had turned as well. We both broke out laughing. It was Eddie Smith, an artist and potter that I had gone to school with back in North Carolina. We hadn't seen each other in a couple of years. We were the only people out on the streets in the Bowery for blocks around, so we stood and talked for about an hour. Another night, things were not as good. As I walked down 4th Street, two guys came out of nowhere and started walking on either side of me, really close. One was black and the other looked Puerto Rican. Both were obviously junkies. They were tall enough for either of them to rest his chin on my head. I hadn't seen anyone else around for a long time. It was late, and lonely—just not lonely enough to suit me. They walked along in silence with me for a minute and then one of them said very quietly, "You got any money?" Now in those days, most of the time if a victim co-operated, nothing violent would happen. The perpetrators just wanted money, and they didn't want trouble about it. So I should have said, "Yes" and given them everything I had. This meant all the quarters and bills that I had stuffed in my front pants pockets from the nights work. I also had an extra, mostly empty wallet, in which I always carried a twenty, just to give to someone in a situation like this. Some muggers didn't like coming up empty. But I froze. "No" is all that came out, and for the life of me I couldn't tell you why. The other guy said, "We're going to check you out." With that, for some reason they simultaneously each reached into my jacket pockets. They each came out with two red-painted wooden billiard balls. I could feel their confusion as we all stood there for a few seconds on the empty street. They sort of looked at each other over my head, and then they each placed the balls back in my pockets. "Sorry to bother you," one of them said, and with that they disappeared into the night. Muggers don't like to bother crazy people because you never know what they are going to do. I figured either they had assumed I was some kind of kook, or they were stoned and the surprise of finding these "toys" just threw them off their purpose.

In the fall of 1970, I went back to college, Lynchburg College, a small liberal arts school in Virginia. I obtained a degree in philosophy in 1972, and then went to Virginia Theological Seminary in Alexandria to study for the Episcopal ministry. During my course of study, I often went out on the streets of Washington to perform for extra money, and sometimes worked for Al Cohen at Al's Magic Shop.

I loved philosophy and theology, but the idea of the ministry didn't appeal to me quite as much. One evening I was doing some magic for the students and faculty at the seminary, and afterwards, Dr. Reginald Fuller, an older, smallish Englishman tapped me on the shoulder. Dr. Fuller was one of the most highly regarded New Testament scholars. He said, "You know, Whitney, when you are doing those card tricks, you light up like a firecracker. It's really something wonderful! Have you ever thought about doing this for a living?" I told him that I really loved magic, but that I felt I wanted to do something 'relevant,' which was a big concept at the time. I meant that I wanted to do something important for the world. He smiled and said, "You know, it's not as if God needs you…" I was stunned, and asked him what he meant. He said that God was quite capable of saving the world himself, and that when He gave someone a talent or gift, a love for something, that was his greatest gift. To make use of one's love for something is a way of investing God's talent. It will make a person happy, and spread joy around to others. He said, "When God needs you for something else, He will call you, and you will want to do it, and you will be happy." I thought a lot about what Dr. Fuller said, and a few weeks later, I dropped out of seminary to go back to performing. I have been on sort of a sabbatical ever since.

My girlfriend at the time was Fran Greenberg, a very talented artist and she and I went to Paris during the spring of 1974. I spent a week or so performing on the Left Bank, and made very good money. I did my act in French, which I had some proficiency in after five years of classes in high school and college. I picked up idiomatic phrases from other street performers around, such as "de votre bon coeur, (from your good heart)" which was how one asked for tips. Street performers were all over the place. One guy ate fire, and specialized in blowouts that would singe the ears of some hapless passerby. Another guy ate a six-foot piece of chain and then brought it up again, a real crowd pleaser. There were lots of musicians from Algeria, the Caribbean and other places. We eventually took off for England, Scotland and Wales. I planned to work the streets when I could to earn extra money, but this didn't work out quite as well as planned. In London, we stayed for a week or two in a squatters building in Earl's Court area. I tried to perform in Hyde Park, but was stopped by the police. I was told that it was an offense to the "Queen", but I really couldn't believe that since she had not even seen my act. At any rate, I tried to perform in Penny Lane and several other locations, but without success.

On a visit to Ken Brooke's Magic Shop, Ken was kind enough to explain that the only people who were allowed to work the streets were disabled vets. He suggested I team up with a performer who was already working legally. "You can pretend you're his son or something." I found my new "father" near Hyde Park. He was an Irishman named Johnny Magoo. He had a fabulous act as a one-man band. The contraption he rolled around in was like several wooden fruit boxes nailed to wheels and peddles. He had drums, a concertina, several horns fixed to pipes, several whistles, a xylophone, a flute, cymbals that fastened to his elbows, and a big drum on his back. Everything was wired and hinged so that he could play almost everything at once. It was quite a show. The carton on the front of this little car had a sign that said "This space to let." Johnny had appeared in the background scene in the opening shot of a Peter

Sellers movie. If you get to see it, you'll get an idea of what he sounded like. He was also a funny and entertaining guy who liked to banter with his audiences.

When I spoke to him about my problem, he immediately began to call a crowd. He introduced me as his son the magician just back from America, and sat back and watched. I did a fairly decent show, and he said that Fran and I should meet him the next day. The next morning the three of us set off for the races. It was Derby day. We performed among the crowd outside the park, and made really good money. We never saw a horse. After that, we spent several days performing with Johnny back in London. We never had a problem with the police, who all seemed to know him. He was a fund of stories about street performers he had known.

Johnny Magoo's great gift was his own good

nature. Many times I saw him return mean spirited jibes with a pleasant self-deprecating joke that almost invariably won a smile from his attacker. He would often apologize to the crowd about the noise he made:

"This isn't the easiest job in London, you understand, but someone's got to do it." "This is an awful racket for sure, but then again, it's worse from where I'm sitting." "It's always the music lovers who complain the most. Now how do explain that?"

After working in London, Fran and I set off for a trip to Wales and Scotland. It was nearly impossible to make any money on the streets then, but we were shown wonderful hospitality by many people. We stayed in bed and breakfast homes and camped out in a small tent when possible.

Going from London to Bath, the countryside is beautiful. We watched the summer solstice at Stonehenge. We then went to Tintern Abbey in Wales, and up the west border area to Birmingham and across toward Oswestry through Iron Bridge.

went to a little village Llanrhaeadr ym Mochnant to

see the legendary falls, and stopped in a little

400 year-old pub one evening in town. The pub was

run by a woman and her mother, and had one

long table where everyone sat and drank. The elder

lady sat by an iron stove that heated the place

and kept feeding the fire. The people from town were

extremely friendly and entertained themselves all

evening with group singing, and when they found out

we were from America, they sang several American

songs. They had incredible voices. I did some magic

for them, and the next thing we knew, black and tans

and malt whiskey were flowing like water. We awoke

in a farm bed the next morning, and the farmer took

us pony-trekking through the hills. I did some magic

for his children that evening at dinner, and then he

took us back to the pub where we had another

ꞓr the drink, night. We woke up

ꞓmeone else's farm. This

ꞁ on kidnapping. A day trip ended up

ꞁ a week.

From there we traveled to Oban, and spent a

week on the island of Iona, one of the most

beautiful, haunting, and haunted isles in the world.

We went up to Inverness, and over to Edinburgh

and Glasgow. After our tour of Scotland, we returned

to London and went back to Paris. Our funds

were extremely low, since we hadn't made any money

in Wales and Scotland, but we expected to clean up

when we got back to Paris. Unfortunately, in Paris,

the tourist season had started, and the police pushed

all the street performers out. Evidently, the café

owners felt that street performers competed for their

customers and had pressed to have them banned

during tourist season. Every time I set up I was

stopped. We had spent our last money on a hotel room, and had none to eat with, and none to get to the airport with. Our plane was leaving in a couple of days, and we were pretty desperate. As we walked back to the hotel one night, I told Fran that something would happen to get us out of the jam. I have always counted on dumb Irish luck to get me out of these situations, Irish luck never gets you the lottery, it just kicks in when you are at the end of the rope and then barely saves you from disaster.

Fran was telling me that I was nuts to count on luck, in terms that would only sound pleasant in French, when I thought I spotted someone across the street that I knew. Running after, I managed to catch up with Robert White. He had been my French professor at Lynchburg College. When I explained our situation, he took us to dinner, and then loaned us enough money to eat on and get to the airport. We made a trip to Virginia a few months later to return the money, and had a delightful dinner at Dr. White's home and told the story of all our adventures.

One of the peculiar things that happened on this trip had to do with my costume. We wanted to wear something in Europe that did not easily identify me as an American. Fran found a beautiful 1930's blue serge double-breasted suit in a thrift shop. It fit me like a glove. To top off the outfit, she found an old Irish gray cloth cap that looked perfect with the suit. In Europe, the outfit was great, and most of the French thought I was an English guy, which sometimes made things a little easier.

The look was sharp, but a little dated and eccentric, plus the suit had wonderful pockets. When I got back to the states, and went out on the streets of Washington, DC to perform again, I found that it was not such a good choice. It looked just like one of the

outfits worn by Robert Redford who played a conman

in the recent hit movie **The Sting**.

I was setting up to perform one night, and an

owner of a store came running out. He yelled

for me to get out or he would call the police. I didn't

understand why he kept saying they didn't need

"my kind of people" around and calling me a grifter. I

wasn't doing any monte or shell game type stuff by

then, and had never heard the word grifter.

When I finally found out what the whole thing was

about, I came up with a new look. I wore

a charcoal gray corduroy coat with a sort of an

English, belted cut, an orange turtleneck shirt and a

gray bowler. This is the outfit that appears in the

photo at the beginning of this book. This should give

some idea of the way life went during my period of

working on the streets as a performer. There are

many other interesting stories and events that would take more than the scope of this work to describe. I thought it might be important to describe things the way they were at that time, so that a full picture of how my point of view on street performing came to be. As I said earlier, there were few models on how to do what I was doing. There weren't any handbooks on the subject. Jeff Sheridan was the only other street performer that I knew of at the time who was doing magic, and if I had seen him work, I suspect I would have totally changed my approach. Years later I met two of the finest street magicians who have ever lived, Jim Cellini and Gazzo and a number of other street magicians. These guys were amazingly more sophisticated street performers than I ever was. Still, I made a living. I learned a lot about performing, and invented the two routines that help me make a living even today, the Mongolian Pop-Knot and the Comedy Four Ring Routine. The idea of this book is to share some of the concepts that I learned the hard way and feel are important and useful for any kind of performing, but especially magic.

ESP Survey

Whenever the weather was too cold to work or too rainy, I found ways to perform and still make money. The first of these came to me when working in New York City. The police had started to give me a hard time, and I needed to keep a lower profile by not drawing the crowds that attracted attention. I bought a *nail-writer* from Tannen's Magic. It is a short piece of pencil lead held in a tiny slip of metal that fastens under the thumbnail and securely holds the lead in place so that you can easily write with the thumb. The apparatus is so small it is hard to notice, plus it is easily hidden behind a small notepad, a pencil or anything else in the hand. It is less noticeable than say a *thumb-tip*. In an emergency, it can be flicked off with a snap of the fingers, and will fly away unnoticed and land someplace where it will never be found. Usually, I would just push it off into my right coat pocket when I needed to get rid of it. I would stand on a busy street, and this worked equally well night or daytime, with a stack of blank business cards in my left hand, wearing the nail-writer and holding a long No 2 pencil in my right hand. As people walked by, I would approach and ask, "Do you believe in extrasensory perception?" I pretended to make a note of their answers on the business cards. It looked as though I was doing some kind of survey. I may have been a student from NYU working on a project. At any rate, eventually someone would stop and ask what I was doing. This is what I waited for, because this person probably was interested in ESP. "I am doing experiments in extrasensory perception," I would say. "Would you mind helping me in a little experiment?" Almost invariably, the individual and his party would agree. "I am going to write down a three digit number on this card, I want you to try and let your mind relax, and not think of anything."

I wrote on the first card of the stack with the pencil, so that the spectators could not see the writing,

"I want you to think of the number:" The stack of cards is held perpendicular to the hand like a deck of cards in dealing position. I left a space for the number near the center of the card. I then exchanged the pencil for the card, and held the card up in the right hand, the pencil and blank cards in my left. "Think of a three digit number, picture it in your mind as if you are looking at it written in the air in front of you. Imagine the numbers are written in bright yellow." I would stare at the card in front of me as if focusing on the number written there. "Can you picture them?"

I waited until the spectator agreed that he could, and then I would let my right hand relax, so that the card was held about waist level, with the back of the hand toward the audience. "There are more than 900 possible three-digit numbers, and you can actually picture one in front of you. If you can see it clearly now, name the first digit?" The spectator would say for example, "Seven." As soon as he named the digit, I would secretly write it on the card with the nail-writer. "Excellent! And now concentrate on the second digit?" I would raise my right hand back up to shoulder level and concentrate on the face of it. "Name the second digit, don't just make it up, picture it. Can you see it?" "Yes." Again my hand would be lowered. "What is it?" I would ask. "Three," the spectator said. I wrote the number with the nail-writer, glancing down at the card if necessary as if to check the number. "Okay, now focus on the third digit. See it in yellow, written in the air in front of you." Again the card is raised so that I can study it, as if sending the picture to them. "Got it?" They would nod, and I would lower the card to waist level. "What is it?" "Nine." I wrote nine on the card with the nail writer and then brought the card back up to shoulder level, and asked, as if checking with the card, "You said seven, three, and nine, correct?" "Yes." Then I would smile and hand them the card to read. "Pretty amazing how well you did with just a little help. Can you spare a little money to help me in my research?" This was almost always worth at least five bucks. Several times, I met people who wanted to know more about what I was doing would offer to take me out for a bite to eat.

Once a psychology professor and his wife took me out for lunch and we had a long discussion about Dr. Rhine and the research at Duke University. The professor wanted me to come speak to his class, and to conduct some tests on me. I politely turned him down. "If I ever go to NYU, I want to be a student, not a subject." I always talked enthusiastically about ESP, but never claimed any special ability. "I just do this little trick when I need money," I told people. The effect was so strong, that on more than one occasion the spectator would just walk off staring at the card in his hand and shaking his head without even hearing my request for scientific research funds. Because I could do this on any street, and did not draw a crowd, the police left me alone. Since I didn't need any particular agility in my fingers for this routine, I could use it when the weather was too cold for anything else. This was especially strong at the time because people were so fascinated by ESP in the late sixties, and there were many stories circulating about Russian military research into psycho-kinesis and telepathy. If I had been more knowledgeable about mentalism at the time, I probably would have developed more similar routines. The success of this gambit did inspire me to work out the walk-around psychic routine that I used for busking in bars in cold weather. This routine featured an original trick called the "Impromptu Card Code," or what later I began to call the "Routine for the Blind." This has been of great use in the years following my career as a street performer, and we will discuss this routine in detail a little later.

Squash!

When the weather was too cold to stand outside for any length of time, I started looking for other places to perform. I tried busking in bars, and found that it was a good alternative to the streets. I started usually by going into a bar and making friends with the bartender. I would show him some magic, and then ask if I could perform for his customers for tips. Since I was providing entertainment for the place and didn't cost anything, this usually worked out fine. One of my favorite tricks at the time was the Abbott's Magic Company effect called *Squash!* This was an incredible feat in which a shot-glass of whiskey is vanished from the hands and reappears behind the performer's knee, still filled with whiskey. It used a pull attached to the back of the shirt or the inside of the jacket near the neck. On the other end of the elastic cord was a rubber ball the size of a golf ball that would hang down under the jacket at the small of the back. The ball is stolen and palmed in the right hand. This would be squeezed into the glass as it was covered between the hands, and with a turn of the body, it would be secretly released so that it could slowly swing under the coat. The pull would bring the glass behind the back under the sport jacket. The ball sealed in all the liquid. The hands would then be outstretched and slowly pressed together and the glass was gone! By reaching back as I pulled the jacket out of the way and pushing with my thumb I was able to release the glass and liquid and slide it down hidden behind my leg, where I could reproduce it from my right knee. I began to use this as an opening trick for the bartender. I wore two pulls with slightly different sized balls so that I could use most common shot glasses. The bigger pull, which I rarely had to use, was a couple of inches shorter, so that I could easily tell which was which, and they could hang one under the other near the small of my back.

I ordered a shot of scotch neat, and when the bartender set it down, I would say, "Want to see something neat? Watch!" and the glass would vanish. I pulled it from behind my knee and set it back on the bar still full of liquid. The bartender and the other customers at the bar would almost always be stunned with amazement. I would immediately ask, "Want to see another one?" and I was into the show. I did cigarettes, sponge balls, a color-changing knife routine, and card and coin tricks. Eventually, I would stop and have a drink, and ask the bartender or manager if I could perform around his tables. Usually, they were happy to let me work as much as I wanted. Two strange incidents involving the *Squash!* trick happened a short time apart. I began using a different method for vanishing the glass, one that was mentioned in the instructions as an alternative. In this method, the right hand covers the glass on a bar or table, inserting the ball, while keeping the elastic hidden under the arm. The left hand slams the bar, as the right hand lets the glass fly under the coat. Both hands then are instantly clapped together and the glass has vanished. This method had more angle problems and less subtle misdirection, but it made up for it in flash and noise. It really got people's attention.

Shortly after I started using this new method, I happened into a bar on the lower East Side. The bartender was about fifty, with a crew cut and service tattoos showing on his bare forearms. He was friendly, but very serious and alert. The bar was a typical neighborhood bar, very much a workingman's bar. It was small and dark even in the daytime, and it was a pretty rough neighborhood. I was the only person at the bar. I asked for a scotch and when he set it down in front of me, I said, "Watch this!" I slammed the bar with my left hand and clapped both hands together. The glass whizzed away perfectly, and I could feel the perfection of the move. Everything was just right, and I knew it. As I looked up at him, his eyes came up from the bar and met mine completely unmoved. The bartender looked me straight in the eye without a trace of reaction. "You want another one?" he asked flatly. Not a sign that anything untoward had happened. I looked at him quizzically, but he stared at me with total frankness, not a trace of irony or humor. I was flabbergasted. I was crushed. I said, "No thanks…" and put a bill on the bar. I walked out into the bright sunlight, blinking and confused. Was he just determined to be unflappable and cool? Perhaps he was an amateur magician and had seen the whole familiar thing coming? How could anybody be so unmoved by such an astounding thing? I knew that he could not have seen how the trick was accomplished, it was as perfect as it could possibly have been. Could he have seen me before in another bar, or heard about my trick from another bartender?

It was a couple of blocks later that I remembered the glass. It was still hanging behind my back under my jacket. I pulled it out, looked at it thoughtfully and then drank the scotch. If the bartender had been as cool as he had seemed, why didn't he ask for his glass back? When I got home, I placed the shot glass on top of my bookcase. It stayed there for a long time to remind me how I had inserted a new 10 on the New York City Blasé Ten Scale.

About a week later, I was in another bar, this time in the West Village area. I was pretty cocky about my magic, and fearless. I knew that if given the chance, the attention of a group, I could stack them up like firewood. I had already gotten past the freak reaction of the bartender from the week before. There were quite sociable people sitting on either side of me, and this bartender was very friendly. In conversation, I mentioned that I was a magician. The bartender said, "Show us a trick." I always looked for just this sort of situation. I stood next to my stool, and ordered a scotch. When it arrived, I noticed that the glass was bigger and heavier than most shot glasses. The sides spread out at wider angle, and the bottom was very thick glass. It was obviously designed to make a shot seem bigger. I didn't worry because I had a larger rubber ball on my second pull that I thought would fit tightly. I looked at the bartender and said, "Okay, you want to see something really neat?" "Shoot, pal." I slowly covered the glass with my right hand. My left hand slammed down on the table and then both hands clapped together. The vanish of the glass was stupendous; as I could tell from the shocked and drop-jawed look on the bartender and everyone on either side of me. I remember this as though it took place in slow motion. As the glass released from my hand and flew under my coat at the speed of light, I stepped back and raised my arms high to show them empty. I took in the looks of surprise all around me, and knew that this was just the beginning. I was going to take this place apart with my magic. At that instant, the glass came whipping around my back and out on the opposite side of my jacket. Its weight, my stepping back too fast, combined with the raising of my arms, somehow let the pull swing around my body and fly out the other side. It didn't seem possible. The jacket should have slowed it down. The glass hit the edge of the bar and dislodged, spilling the whiskey. As I grabbed for the tumbling glass, I knocked it right past the bartender and it cracked the mirror behind the bar. In the process it sprayed the bartender, the spectators and me with a fine mist of Johnny Walker dew. The ball on the end of the pull was flapping back and forth caught on my jacket. Everyone was stunned for a second until the whole thing—effect, method, disaster—all became crystal clear. Then everyone began to laugh. The bartender said, "I hope that's not your best trick." There was nothing left to do but laugh. I turned to him and said, "I think I would like another one..." And he set down a new scotch. This one I drank. After a few minutes, I caught my breath and was able to do some more magic, and everyone was pleased. The bartender told me to come in for a couple of hours on Saturday nights for the rest of the month and entertain his customers, and he would forget about the mirror. This was what I had wanted anyway. So the whole experience wasn't a total waste. I haven't performed *Squash!* since, even though I still think it is a wonderful trick. When I use an elastic pull or a reel as in *Ring-Flite* nowadays, I let it go smoothly and slowly like I had done in the past with *Squash!* Subtlety has its advantages. The pull becomes like a third hand that slips out of the jacket and quietly slips something away, an adjunct to the sleight-of-hand instead of a replacement. I managed to survive this catastrophe and many more embarrassments, faux pas, accidents, and stupidities over the years. Polish only comes from being ground down. But the important thing is to have a positive attitude to these experiences. We are always growing. We rarely are caught short the same way twice. Every time something like this happens, and it happens less and less as experience and skill grows, we can take heart that that is one more lesson we have past and will not need to repeat. Magicians are always standing just a broken thread away from calamity and humiliation. Even so humility is both a profitable and an endless study.

The Impromptu Card Code: A Routine for the Blind

Busking in a bar in New York City back in the late Sixties was not easy. For one thing, New Yorkers are very toughened against strangers and are always looking for the angle or scam that might be played on them. For a second thing, close-up magic was something that was not very familiar to people. People thought of magic as children's entertainment. On the West Coast, the **Magic Castle** was beginning to create a following for sophisticated sleight-of-hand, but in the eastern United States this was still a sell. Sometimes I think we forget what an important and beneficial influence on our art the **Magic Castle** has been. By helping to make magic the favorite entertainment of Hollywood celebrities, the club that Bill and Milt Larsen built helped forge a new image for all magicians. Going up to a table in a bar or restaurant in New York in those days and asking the customers if they would like to see "some magic" or a "card trick" or "something neat" would often bring the response "Get lost." After knocking around at this for a while, I thought about how effective the ESP Survey had been at catching people's interest. I started looking for a way to apply mentalism to table-hopping. I found that if I came to a table and asked "Would you mind helping me in a little experiment in extrasensory perception?" the chances were much better for a positive response. I had a few store-bought mental tricks like *Mental Choice*, *Brainwave*, and a few little packet tricks with mental themes or that used Dr. Rhine's ESP deck. Some sleight-of-hand tricks with cards could be turned into ESP themes, and there were several different versions of Paul Curry's *Out of this World* that I liked. If Uri Geller had been familiar in the States at that time, spoon-bending and other psycho kinesis demonstrations would have been perfect, as would have been invisible thread tricks. but the magic community was just beginning to explore the uses of invisible thread, and I was not really very well connected back then. I muddled along, and eventually came up with a fairly decent routine that brought in good money just hustling tips in bars and restaurants. I dressed like a typical college student, and came up to a table as if conducting a sociology or psychology experiment. I would try certain tests with each person at a table, and as the results of the tests became more and more incredible, I would lighten the approach and make a few jokes. The spectators became enchanted with what was fast-becoming a little ESP magic show. The audience was charmed, had fun and didn't mind when I inevitably ended each session with a grin and, "You guys got any money you can spare for my research?"

At some point, I stumbled onto the idea that

became the centerpiece of the routine. I found that I could use an old method, to signal a partner under the table in a poker game using a foot tap, as a simple code for the suits and values of the cards. The essential new idea was that I discovered how to teach the code to the spectator right in front of the others. I developed what became the *Impromptu Card Code*, a two-person mind reading act that used an instant stooge from the audience.

I had already played with the idea of instant stooges as I improvised magic at bars that I worked regularly. I found that I could get a friendly spectator's attention and with a wink and a significant flash of the bottom card of the deck, could compromise his loyalty to the rest of the group. I would then force a card on another spectator, and then have him hold it without looking at it or showing it to anyone. I then asked my "stooge" to concentrate, blank his mind, and let pictures of cards float by in his imagination. "When some card seems to dominate your view, name it." He would name the card I had flashed to him. When the chosen card was revealed, it matched! I would congratulate the psychic and give him all the credit. We would repeat the experiment, as I again flashed him the bottom card before forcing it on someone else. The third time, I would surreptitiously flash him the bottom card as I asked him to go out of the room so that there was no way "he could be sent any signals." A card was selected, and I told the spectators to call him back and ask him what it was. Another miracle. Each time a card was forced, I tried to use a different method. I used a classic force, a *Hindu Shuffle Force*, the "marking the cut" ruse, Harry Lorayne's *Fan Force*, etc. Eventually this routine became both familiar and popular for the regulars, and they started cueing each other. I would send a regular spectator out of the room with a "new" spectator to accompany him, so that we could be sure that the "psychic" wasn't getting any help. This guy would now tip the secret to the guard, who would then be able to name the chosen cards. After a short while it became a scam that was played on newcomers. Everyone would go out one at a time and name the correct card, always acting as if they had no clue how it was being accomplished. The regulars were aware that I was forcing cards, but didn't know how I managed to do it, and they found this very impressive. It wasn't long before I could even stop forcing cards. I would flash the bottom card to the psychic who would then leave the room, and then to another "player." I could shuffle the pack and hand it to the second player and he would "freely" choose a card, the card I flashed him! Finally, the "sucker" newcomer would go out, and we would all agree that whatever card he named we would pretend that that was it. He would now be totally at a loss for explanations, and the regulars thought the whole thing was great fun. Sometimes I would turn a card face-up in the deck for the "sucker" to name, and when he came back and named his card it was the correct one. This would drive everyone in the room nuts, since when I turned my back and secretly turned over a card, I would just switch decks for an *Invisible Pack* deck. I sometimes varied this by using a *Brainwave Deck* so that the chosen card was from a different pack! By constantly changing methods and taking advantage of any lucky coincidences, I could keep everyone fooled and entertained.

It was this fooling around that gave me the idea for the *Impromptu Card Code*. This is how it looked to the spectators. I would walk up to a table, ask for help in some ESP experiments and then when I got a positive response I would sit down at the table. I took out a deck of cards and had them examined and shuffled. I turned to one of the spectators and asked him what the odds are that he could name the color of a card I held up with its back to him. He would agree that it was fifty-fifty. I said, "I am going to go through this deck one card at a time, and I want you to name the color of the card—black or red." As I held up each card, he would call out its color. He was right every time. We would go through about twelve or fifteen cards, and then after he called a card "Red," I would ask "Diamond or Heart." He named Heart and was again correct. I asked, "What is the value of the card?" and he named "The four." At that point I picked up all the cards and commented on what an accomplished psychic he was. Everyone at the table is bedazzled. They knew that this guy and I had never met, often they were all from out of town, either tourists or businessmen in for a meeting and therefore they could not see how we could have had a secret code. But there was no other explanation! The secret is simplicity itself. When I first sat down, I would try to get the spectator's complicity with conspiratorial winks and nudges as I explained what I was going to do, and how it would look to his companions. I always described it in such a way that he could visualize how impressive he would look, and what a good gag it would be to play on his friends. "I am going to go through this deck, one card at a time, while you will call out the color, either red, or black. You will visualize a color in your mind and then name it. It is as simple as that. Can you imagine what an astonishing and wonderful thing it would be if you named every card correctly? In your mind, try to see yourself naming every card correctly, and what an impact it would make on everyone around.

"I believe that if we can establish a certain kind of *rapport*, we will be able to do just that, and really amaze all your skeptical friends. Are you with me? You understand what everyone expects of you? You will use your ESP to read my mind and name the color of each card. If this works, it will blow everyone away. If you can tell the red cards..."

At this point I would give him a significant look, as my foot was pressed once firmly on his foot under the table. As I continued, "from the black cards (I pressed his foot twice and smiled at him) it would be evidence of incredible psychic ability," "Do you get it? All you do is name the cards red (pressing his foot again one time) or black (pressing his foot twice). Are you with me?" I waited for some look or sign that he was following the concept and would play along. It is important that I get agreement of some kind from the stooge before I begin. It is essential that he understand that I am conspiring with him against the others, he can't think that I am trying to subliminally influence him. It has to be clear that I mean to signal him, and expect him to co-operate with me in a sort of scam on the others. By painting a picture of what it will look like to the others, I can get him to want to play this little prank on them.

"Let's give it a try."

I would fan the cards in front of me, and then pull out one at a time—holding it so that its back was to the "psychic." I would always caution him not to call the card until it was all the way out of the pack, so that I couldn't cheat by pulling out the color after he called it. After all, we want to play fair…

As he began naming the cards red or black, the excitement in the room would grow. I would look at various spectators with surprise or an amused shake of the head at each correct call, in an

attempt to keep their attention above the table. Each
card would be tossed onto the table face-up, red
in one pile, black in the other.

After about fifteen cards are called, I would
select a low card such as a four or a five. I would
signal the color. When he named "Red," I would ask,
"Is it a heart (tapping his foot) or a diamond
(no tap)." He would say, "Hearts."
"Can you tell me the value of the card?" I tapped his
foot five times. "Five of Hearts?" he would call. I threw
the card face-up on the table and shook his hand.
"You have a real gift."
The routine that eventually developed around this
trick was fun. I would usually be secretly
setting the deck up for Paul Curry's *Out of this World*
as I chose cards to hold up. I would pick up the pack
of discarded black cards on the table and put it on top
of the pack, and the red cards would be placed to the

bottom of the pack—so that the deck was divided completely into red and black.

Then I would perform *Out of this World* with a second spectator. This always zapped the first spectator because he couldn't for the life of him figure out how I was signaling the second spectator, since I would pace around the table as the second spectator separated the cards into piles.

I would do some other mental effect with each of the other spectators at the table, usually finishing with *Brainwave* or the *Invisible Pack* done as a psychic effect. At the end of the ten to fifteen minute routine I would thank everyone for his participation and ask with a grin, "Do you guys have any money you can spare for my research?" As I collected the tips I would say, "You probably figured out that this is not really ESP. See if you can wrangle the secrets of everyone else's tricks from them without giving up your own…"

I always imagined the conversation after I left would go like this:

First spectator (stooge), "So how did that thing work?"

Second spectator, "I don't know, how did you do yours?"

First spectator (thinking the second spectator is lying through his teeth), "…I don't know."

I don't know if this is how it usually went, but it sure was fun thinking that it did. I know that they talked about this routine for a long time. The bartenders said that this act always seemed to sell a lot of drinks as the group tried to figure out exactly what had happened to them. I had somehow stopped pulling this thing for many years, until one night in the summer of 1980 something happened that forced me to resurrect this routine in an entirely new way, and with a surprising twist. Overnight, *The Impromptu Card Code* became *The Routine for the Blind*.

I was working in a restaurant in Long Beach, California called Marie Callenders. As I went around the tables, I came up to a table with two couples. It was obviously a twenties-something couple and the parents of one or the other. I asked them if they would like to see some magic, and they enthusiastically agreed.

As I started the performance, I had the elder lady take a card and then turned to the younger lady and said, "And would you take a card..."

She did not react at all, so I repeated the request. She said, "Are you speaking to me? I'm sorry. I'm blind. I didn't know."

At that moment I realized that she had a seeing-eye dog lying quietly next to her.

"No, I'm sorry. I tell you what. This trick may not mean so much to you, so I will let someone else take the card and finish this one. Then I would like to try something special with you.

Is that okay?"

She said fine. I finished the trick thinking all the time, "What am I going to do for her?"

Once before, in a retirement home I had attempted to do the sponge balls for a blind man, thinking that he would enjoy feeling them seem to grow in his hand. What I didn't count on was that he couldn't see what I was doing, so every time I tried to put something in his hand he wanted to feel and check it out. I couldn't get away with anything. He was real proud of himself. He said, "It's harder to cheat a blind man that you'd think." This made me laugh really hard.

Now what could I do with this blind lady? As the card trick seemed to finish on its own, I turned to Lynda and sat down next to her. Reaching for a long shot, I asked, "Do you believe in ESP?"

She said, "I don't know."

"You know it has been sometimes theorized that people who have lost one faculty often make up for it in others. That blind people might be more sensitive to other influences for example. I'd like to do something here just for fun. I want to test your ESP. It will be really easy. You are going to do things that will make everyone else at the table wonder. I have a deck of cards in my hand.

Do you play cards?" She nodded.

"Good. I will spread the cards out facing me with their backs to you. I'm going to pull a card out one at a time, and you are going to call it either 'red' or 'black.' Since there is a fifty-fifty chance that you will call it correctly, we should expect you to get about half right. If you could do a lot better than that—and if we establish a certain rapport I think you can—this would explain a lot about you to your family here." As I talked, I squeezed her forearm reassuringly. Then I said okay, here's what's going to happen. I'll pull out a card and you will call it either 'red' (I pressed her foot lightly once) or 'black.' (I pressed her foot twice). Got the idea?"

She could barely repress her smile. She said, "Got it."

Well, we went through the deck and she named the cards red and black perfectly through about twenty cards. She didn't need to see the looks on her parents faces, she could hear them gasping and hyperventilating. When she called the suit and then the value, Lynda's mother said to her, "I'm never going to play cards with you again!"

Lynda just laughed. I told her, "Let's keep going…" By this time I had the deck set up for *Out of this World*. I'm going to put one card on the table face up here to your left, and another card face up to the right. I placed her hand on one, then the other.

"This is the red card, and this is the black card. I'm going to hand you the deck face down,

and I want you to put the top card to your right if it's red, and to the left if you think it's black. Go by your first impression. Trust me, you are going to do really well."

I false shuffled the deck and handed it to Lynda. She did as instructed, but without the same self-confidence as before. At the reveal, I said, "Now Lynda, you won't be able to see how you did,

but you will certainly hear how you did as I show everyone the cards. You were perfect! You didn't miss one card!"

Now the parents and her husband were visibly shaken. Lynda was having a good time.

Luckily, I always carry *Brainwave Deck* when I am working close-up.

"Lynda, it's the strangest thing. I had a dream last

night that a mysterious lady came up to me and handed me a card. I dreamt that I took the card and hid it in a deck of cards that I always kept by the bed. When I woke up, I put the deck in my pocket. I've carried it around all day, and this is it.

Lynda, what is the name of the card that the mysterious lady gave me?"

Lynda smiled. "Jack of Hearts."

I said, "You are not going to believe this, but as I go through the deck very slowly so that I can't do anything sneaky, one card is face-up in the pack. You can tell it's the Jack of Hearts by the applause. But look! The Jack of Hearts is from an entirely different deck! It must have come from that mysterious lady."

Two weeks later Lynda and her husband sent me a deck of Braille playing cards and a nice note. Her parents were still nervous around her. This was one of the most fun magic shows I have ever done, and it still warms me to think about how cool it was to fall into cahoots with a perfect stranger and pull a fast one on her family—just for fun. I put this routine and story in my lecture notes in 1982, and it has been a part of my lecture ever since. Twice in the last twenty years similar situations have arisen in my close-up performing. This routine played perfectly each time. Over the years more than a dozen magicians have told me how well this has worked for them, and what a great way it is to handle what would otherwise be a difficult situation.

This past summer (2001), my good friend Brian Gillis brought down the house in the Parlor of Mystery at the **Magic Castle** with the *Routine for the Blind*. He and his partner Sue have one of the most incredible two-person mind reading acts around. On this night, a blind man was sitting on the front row with a group of friends. It was Stevie Wonder. The Parlor stage is

level with the first row of the audience. Brian was able

to walk up to Wonder and enlist him in the gag

because the front row of seats hid their feet from the

rest of the audience, and the people sitting on the

front row were looking at their two faces.

When Stevie Wonder named the value of the last

card, the audience cheered as he stood up

and turned around and took a prizefighter's bow.

This story of the blind girl and the magician was

reprinted with my permission in a book on

public speaking with magic. The author's version of

the story was a bit fanciful—he had this take

place with a little blind girl named Wendy, for

example—and his description of the method did not

include all the psychological principles that were

necessary for it to work. This would be a problem

for anyone who tried to perform the routine from this

description. For one thing, I would rarely try
this with a blind child, or a very old blind person.
The communication skills required and the concepts
being communicated are subtle. Any
misunderstanding will spoil the whole thing, and it is
probably difficult enough to communicate with
a stranger secretly in front of others—especially a
blind person—without having to deal with the
distractions and conceptions of a child, or the focus of
a very elderly person. However, each situation is
unique, and the right rapport with an individual might
make me give it a shot.

One has to be careful with a lady, so that the action of
tapping does not seem too intrusive,
and so that one is not marring or scuffing an
expensive satin shoe.

Later the author submitted his version of the story to
Chicken Soup for the Soul #3 without

checking with me. The method was tipped along with the story. I was very miffed, and when the television series *Chicken Soup for the Soul* wanted to present this story, I insisted that it be done in a manner that did not reveal the secret. They were able to do this, and magician/actor George Tovar played the part of the magician.

A1 Multimedia put out the video **Convention at the Capital - Live 2000**. In this video is my performance of the *Routine for the Blind* with a volunteer from the audience and the description of the method—both from my lecture during the convention. I have to admit that my description of the routine is a bit windy, but the performance could be helpful to those interested in seeing how the agreement with the spectator is established. Print is cold. Certain nuances are better grasped from seeing it in performance.

The description in this booklet is the most comprehensive I have made because it traces the development of the routine. I hope that by following the thinking that went into this development,

the reader can get a better concept of how to go about the business of setting up rapport and getting agreement from the stooge.

When something goes wrong, it can go very wrong. I know of one performer who tried to use

his knee against a blind girl's knee. She thought he was trying to play footsie with her. This was because he had not adequately prepared her for what he was attempting to do. It must have been

quite a delicate situation.

In his column *Confessions of a Road Warrior* in the September 2001 **Genii Magazine**, David Acer tells a very funny story of madcap magician David Williamson's. David Williamson had remembered the

Routine for the Blind and tried to use it with an elderly blind man. He had evidently handed the old man the deck to separate himself, and this may have been a distraction. It is much better to do the handling of the cards as we have described so that the stooge has nothing else to think about. If Acer's description is accurate, Williamson only tapped for one color—red—signally black by doing nothing. This makes it more difficult for the stooge to catch on to the idea. One tap for red and two for black is much more obvious, and more obviously a code, and may be safer. We want things to be clear to the stooge, and as quickly as possible.

Here is David Acer's description:
"Now remember—place the black cards to your right and the red (tap tap) cards to your
left...black cards on the right, red (tap tap) on your left. Got it?"
And Grandpa said, "Yeah, yeah—I
got it. Hey, who the hell is kicking my foot?" And that was the end of that.

This is a very funny story, although I am sure it was

not a lot of fun at the time. There may have been a mistake in the way the code was set up, or it could be that the old man was just not going to co-operate anyhow. Those things happen. But it seems to me it is usually worth the risk to try it.

When this connection succeeds, the magician comes away as a real hero who has surmounted what everyone in the audience can see could have been a difficult problem. Even more important, the magician has made a star out of the blind person, and they have had a secret little game together that neither is likely to forget.

The best way to prepare for this routine is to go over the wording that we've presented here carefully. It isn't necessary to use the exact words, but it is important to understand the steps that the performer goes through in order to make his meaning clear and establish an understanding with the stooge. Common

sense and a sense of humor will go a long way.
The routine should be fairly easy for almost any
magician, and just having it in the back of
the mind is a great way to prepare for the day when
the appropriate situation arises.

The Lessons of the Street

At this point, I want to speak about the many
important lessons that can be learned from the
performers who operate in the last great, live and
unstructured venue—the streets, fairs and
marketplaces of the world. There are many things that
any performer working in any venue can learn
from those who have to deal with the "madding
crowd" of the open places.

The most important skill for the street performer is to
call and hold an audience. Stopping busy people and
gathering a crowd isn't easy, and it takes some
thought and lots of brass. For most magicians, in the

majority of performing situations, calling a crowd isn't that important a skill. Usually, we walk out and there they are—like sitting ducks—waiting for us.

But in some situations, it can be an invaluable ability. Performing walk-around at a corporate function, and working a trade show booth are good examples. These are situations in which the performer has to ring in his *tip*, or crowd.

In these rare situations, the secrets of the street performer can be worth their weight in gold.

But knowing how to hold a crowd is the same in every performing situation, and the street performer is also the master of this skill. When I am performing, I still feel that the crowd is about to walk away and that I have to do something to hold them in their seats. I work the audience with that in mind, and even though I know they won't actually get up from their seats and leave, I want to hold them mesmerized in the same manner as I did when my audiences were quite able and willing to vote with their feet.

We should consider what the street performer goes through, both in calling and holding a crowd, and then see how it might apply to other situations in which the performer's work holds less stringent demands.

First, how do you get up the nerve to stop the passersby? I used to stand on a spot for a long time until I felt I owned the place. After that, everyone else was just visiting. It was my stage, and I belonged there. This is a very powerful technique. Before an important performance, I still like to open the curtains and walk the stage in an empty house until I feel that the space belongs to me. You'll be surprised at how much this can alleviate stage fright. But it can also help put the performer "in the zone" before a show. Thinking through your opening gambit beforehand is essential. After that, the performer has to know what he will do each step of his show before he goes out. Improvisation should only come when he already has a totally worked-out script to fall back on. He must know his patter and tricks backwards and forwards. With practice and memorization comes confidence. And we need lots of confidence to overcome our natural fear of the unknown. The more prepared we are for the situation, the more comfortable we will be. This helps to ease the fear that comes when we suddenly have to interrupt those around us with the call. "Hey, hey, hey! Ladies and Gentlemen. Come here and watch the most astounding feat you will ever see."

A performer should view the crowd as individuals, not as some mob that has no face. The audience should be addressed and spoken with, not spoken to. When we look at one individual at a time, instead of everyone and no one at once, it is much more controllable and comfortable. Each line that the performer utters should be directed at an individual in the crowd. The performer speaks personally to one person, waits for acknowledgement or agreement, and turns to another to make his next point. This is vastly superior to the common manner of most beginning speakers and entertainers who look out into their audiences and speak as if the crowd were some huge many-headed beast that has to be addressed. By looking over the heads of the crowd or focusing his attention at some vanishing point in the middle of the group, the neophyte hopes to avoid being frightened by the monster he can't seem to face. By focusing instead on individuals, the "monster" becomes just a bunch of individual people like those we speak to every day.

Looking at an individual when we deliver a line not only makes the performance seem more intimate and interesting, it relieves some of the fear that comes from facing a group. Even on stage in a theater, where the audience is draped in darkness, I pretend that I can see individuals and am addressing and getting a nod or smile from each one. Finally, we train ourselves to experience stage nerves positively. It is after all, just the old "fight or flight syndrome" which is in operation. Adrenaline and other drugs created by our bodies are being unleashed in order to prepare us to respond to some ill-perceived threat.

Instead of thinking of these as "butterflies in the stomach," we should look at them as useful chemicals for the performer to have, since they give us the energy and clarity of mind to face the challenge of mounting the bench. Instead of preparing us to fight or run from an enemy, they prepare us to face the odd beast that is a crowd of strangers.

Next, how do we get our potential audience to come over and watch the things we want to show them? By the way, don't go up to people and ask them, "Would you like to see something?" as David Blaine did in his first television special. This is not going to be very productive in most situations. If you have a video crew following you, people might respond as they did for Blaine, otherwise you will be told to buzz off, or even much, much worse. One method is to use some silent, non-threatening skill that can attract people over to watch. This needs to be something that the performer can keep going until he gets a crowd together. Juggling, unicycle, card flourishes, billiard ball productions and mime are all good examples. At trade shows, I like to use the shell game, fast and loose, or three-card monte to accomplish the same thing. We need only to picture one of the classic street performers from the turn of the century, the organ grinder, to see the power of a live animal to draw a crowd. We can't even picture the hurdy29 gurdy without the monkey. An appearing rabbit, a trained dog, a cobra-killing mongoose, a talking parrot or "mind-reading" goat can collect a crowd faster than any human. Gazzo says that it is common wisdom among street performers that "you can't compete with a monkey man." In Paris, Phillipe Petit (who later walked the wire between the World Trade Center buildings in New York and became a Ringling Brothers' star) used to do slack wire, and setting up the equipment would attract interest. Then he would circle around with a long piece of rope, finally laying it down to mark out his performance space. The entire process was done in silence, and was an automatic draw for a crowd. "What's he going to do?" As people came closer to see, they formed themselves around the rope circle into an audience.

This rope circle became a sacred space, and any violation was punished by the immediate cessation of the show until the unwitting spectator stepped back out of the circle. So, the crowd was called in silence by the very process of creating a performing space. This was both economical and efficient. A time-honored method of the street performer is to simply "call" a crowd. The performer begins by addressing everyone in hearing distance. He promises to show miracles, and gets everyone laughing: "Step right up ladies and gentlemen. I'm about to demonstrate some miracles of crafty science that you will be talking about for the next several weeks. In fact, you will be telling your grandchildren about this day when…"

This is followed by some come-on—often a false promise that turns out to have absolutely no connection to the actual performance—that will draw interest and attention such as:

1) "You saw the deadly poisonous snakes from the wet jungles of South America, which I keep locked away in this very basket..."

2) "I took a woman from the audience stood her on her head and spun her like a top..."

3) "This thirty-foot length of rope sailed into the air before your very eyes, yes indeed, the fabulous Hindu mystery of the Indian rope trick..."

4) "You had a chance to win this $100 bill just by explaining a simple mystery..."

I remember a carnival "auctioneer" for an "advertising" truck (a jam auction) who would pull a kid on stage and wrap a hundred dollar bill in a handkerchief. He told the kid to hold the folded bandana tightly and not move. He then would promise to make the hundred-dollar bill vanish under these impossible conditions and re-appear in an envelope that was nailed to the wooden post at the side of the stage.

"I will then give that same $100 bill to anyone in the audience who can explain how this miracle was accomplished." He went into his standard sales routine after drawing the crowd he wanted, and at the end, he took back the handkerchief from the kid who had been standing on the side of the stage through the whole affair. He gave the kid some little prize and said that he had received a signal from the boss man that he had run out of time for this show, and would have to do the trick at the next performance, which would be starting in "just a few minutes."

Calling a crowd is often made easier if the talker (the one who ballyhoos the act) and the performer are two different people. This is one of the most effective, and certainly the least intimidating, method of starting a show for the performer. It is hard to sell yourself. Having someone do it for you is a blessing. If that person also takes charge of leading applause and passing the hat, the take will be invariably larger. During the last couple of years of my street-performing career, I would put signs up around the performing area that would announce the show and attract interest. These sometimes, but not always, announce a show time, and can be a tremendous help in drawing a crowd. The "Next Show 1:15" type sign is extremely common among magicians in the trade show setting. Intriguing props and costume can also be helpful. Another method is to start with a trick that is small—effective only for one or two people— and then continue performing until a crowd is gathered. The performer only has to stop one or two people, or a small group that is walking together and get them to watch something. A setup can be very effective for this. The performer pretends to be taking a survey or something, and then when he gets someone to stop, he inveigles him into watching a trick—as in the ESP Survey we described above. Once he has their attention, he begins performing with a louder and broader style in order to attract others over to watch. He builds up the crowd as he moves to larger and more theatrical tricks.

The use of "boosters" can be extremely powerful. A booster is a shill who pretends to be just a spectator. One or more partners can play the part of an audience to get the crowd started. They react with great interest and enthusiasm so as to draw other people over to see the show in progress. The *Shell Game* and *Three-Card Monte* are almost always done this way. But it can be a valuable technique in many performing situations. I have used the company's sales people in a trade show booth to act in this fashion, and usually they enjoy being part of a scam to draw a crowd. *Fast and Loose* (*Endless Chain*) is one of the repeatable tricks I often use with boosters at a trade show to start a tip (draw a crowd). People are attracted to money, to anything that looks like gambling, and to anything that seems to be creating excitement from "fellow folk."

Once the crowd begins to gather, it is important to establish a performance space. On a sidewalk or in a narrow trade show aisle, a booster can stand at a certain distance from the performer so that the crowd will form around him. The distance is always as great as possible, but that is still too close for the passersby to comfortably walk between.

By forcing the traffic to slow down and go around the performer's shill, a performance space is established at the same time the crowd is slowed down and forced to notice something is happening, thus helping to build the "tip." This works especially well on a sidewalk because the street becomes a barrier on the other side of the shill.

I often use the spectators themselves to create the space. The performer has someone put his foot on a card or has two spectators hold a net as in one of the *Balls in the Net* routines. This creates a space between the performer and the spectators whose positions are now "frozen." The performer steps back away from the spectator, thus establishing a performing area. This makes it difficult for traffic to move through the space, and as people slow down to get past; they can't help but be drawn into the show.

I use my published routine, *The Chicago Surprise*, in this way quite often. A blue-backed card is dropped to the floor, and a spectator is asked to put his foot on it. This card eventually will change into the chosen card. At a cocktail party, reception or hospitality room, this works like a charm. A performer can also use props (such as a table or tray, a rug, a platform to stand on, or a rope spread in a circle as Phillipe Petit used) to create a space for the performance.

Now that the audience has been called and the performance space set up, the street performer must endeavor to keep the crowd together and entertained. What does it take to hold them? First, the street magician does routines—never tricks. Every time something comes to an end, it is a chance for someone to leave. Often the spectators are busy people with places to go and things to do. They feel spellbound by the performer, and can't leave in the middle of the story. The first time something is completed, they will try to duck before he sucks them in again. So the street performer wants to keep every routine going as long as possible. He tries to turn these into one seamless overall routine that lasts right up to the moment he hits them with the request

for money. Or, as in the trade show situation, the

moment he might sock them with his advertising

pitch.

The dangerous times are when something is over and

the performer needs to put equipment away, or get

something out. There can never be a dead space.

Whenever something is being put away, he tries to be

taking something else out with the other hand. The

eyes never leave the crowd. The patter never wavers.

Failing to take this into consideration is one of the

rankest indications of an amateur and inexperienced

performer. One good method is to be starting a hook

line for the next routine as soon as the first routine

is over. While the performer is putting away or setting

up he uses lines that the spectator can't walk

away from:

"Have you ever seen a Tribble?"

"Do you believe in ghosts?"

"I want to show you the strangest device that Houdini ever tried to escape from…"

"Next, someone in this group is going to have a chance to win a valuable prize…"

"I have a hundred dollar bill right here that says…"

"In this bag is a restraint made for the criminally insane. You may wonder why I have it…"

"I'm going to let the goose (monkey, parrot, ferret, horse) perform the next effect…"

When I see inexperienced magicians performing in the *Close-Up Gallery* at the **Magic Castle**, the lack of these smooth segues from one trick to another is the most common fault. The tyro will sometimes finish an effect, take his applause and then bend behind the table to put his props away and grab something else out of his bag. I often fantasize that when he gets back up to his seated position, the entire room would be empty—it might have helped him to realize his mistake—for the audience is already walked off mentally.

Roving eye contact throughout the performance is absolutely essential. Every spectator should be fixed with a smile and a look. Drawn in. Conspired with. Winked at. Seduced. Kidded. Suckered. Laughed at. Humored. Something. Anything. Just make it personal between the performer and each spectator. People are transfixed by the personal. Friendly traffic with a person who has the attention of a group is a powerful magnet. Human emotion is the most intriguing and attention-attracting weapon the performer has at his disposal. Every chance possible, the performer should display some sort of feeling, the more intense the better. We should study our magic routines with an eye focused on seeking out those interactive situations that might provoke an emotion from the performer.

These are often built into the trick itself. We can discover our line of presentation through Examining the nature of the routines we want to perform. Let the trick inform our presentation. For example, some effects invoke a challenge to the spectator, or contain some element like "the magician in trouble." These are gold to be mined. Anger. Fear. Discomfort. Laughter! Disgust. Perplexity. Cunning. Deep thought. Relief! Excitement. Enthusiasm. Bravery. Surprise! Sincerity. Seriousness. Delight! Love. Pain. Nervousness. Victory! Read through these again, picturing situations in a magic show that might inspire these feelings in the performer.

Doesn't it grab your attention just reading the names of these feelings? Think how powerful watching someone else go through the actual experience might be. That is what theater is all about, and magicians should make use of all the techniques of acting and theater that they can command.

These are the borrowed weapons that we use in our craft.

Even very course acting that only mimics these feelings is more entertaining than a mere declamatory style. On the street, we especially need all of these tactics to draw and hold the attention of an audience. Think how more powerful these weapons could be in a tamer, more controlled performing situation. We magicians should learn how to "act." Reading some of the classic texts in acting, taking a course in acting, or participating in improvisational acting groups—these are all extraordinarily useful. After all, we are supposedly "actors playing the part of a magician."

Personally, I have always felt that that famous quote from Robert-Houdin was absolutely true, but a practically worthless maxim for most magicians. The reason is that most magicians are not trained as actors, and therefore haven't got a clue what it means to be an actor, or to "play a magician." If magicians were conversant with the technique of the actor, they would understand how to organically live the part as if the actions of the performer and his byplay with the spectators were just as a real magician would experience them. They would have a line of attack on the problem.

As it works in practice, the average magician is left with the same wretched approach that an amateur and untrained actor would take; e.g., to mimic the speech and mannerisms of what they picture a magician to be—to do an "impression" of a magician. This produces the stilted and mechanical figure that so many (man, how I hate this term) "lay people" have come to think of as a magician.

The trained actor would first try to figure out what it would be like if he himself had magic powers, and why he would be displaying them to an audience. Why am I doing this for these people? How long have I had these powers? What do they mean to me? Am I proud of these abilities? Bored with them? Do I want to hide the fact that these powers are real, and let people think of them as tricks? Am I trying to convince people magic powers such as mine truly exist? Instead of *imitating* the image of a magician he might have in his head, the true actor tries to *invent* a magician by getting in touch with the back story, motivations, and conflicts that a "real" magician might experience. He imagines the character in response to the situation and conditions he faces—he plays the part within its story.

To learn the technique of the actor as it would apply to the improvisational situations that a magician faces, I highly recommend Viola Spolin's books, *Improvisation for the Theater*, and *Theater Games for the Lone Actor*. These are a gold mine for any performer, and teach the skills and theory needed in a simple, fun way. They utilize the concept of games, and have exercises which are designed to let the student discover for himself the meaning and application of controlling focus, freedom, point of concentration and so forth, while all the time encouraging the organic process of discovery. These books are especially valuable to anyone who works with a partner, but are important for all performers, even those who work alone. What two or more actors do with each other on the stage, is very similar to what any variety performer does with his audience.

Actors are taught to work with each other as if holding on to a rope. Sometimes one actor is pulling, and the other is being pulled. Then the second actor pulls the rope, and the first is being dragged around. The rope must never go slack. This image is useful in understanding how the focus of the audience is taken and given by the actors. Usually, an actor does not directly address or interact with the audience itself. In Shakespeare, the characters often break from the scene and address the audience directly in soliloquy. This is, I think, partly because the theater of Shakespeare's day was not very far removed from the traveling bands of jongleurs and actors who performed outdoors for the people in the square. But this is rare in most stage acting today. In variety performance, the audience becomes the other end of the rope. Many performers act as if they needed to tame the audience, like a lion tamer. They don't allow for the audience to have any part in the performance other than as spectators. Using heckler lines and a heavy barrage of patter, they intimidate and overwhelm the audience out of fear of losing control of the performance situation.

Much more exciting and fun is the performer who can control the situation organically, letting the audience play and interact with him. He maintains control by keeping the rope taut, not by constantly dragging the audience around. Imagine two dogs playing "pull it" with a rope. Neither tries very hard to win. They enjoy the process. The stronger dog will let the weaker dog drag him around for a while, and then he drags the weaker. The strong dog doesn't want the weak dog to lose interest and quit. They enjoy the process, instead of constantly seeking to win a competition. This is play. No one likes being dragged around for very long. In the same way, the performer should let the audience interact as much as possible without letting the rope go slack, or having it jerked out of his hands. Not every audience member who interjects something in a performance is a heckler. Most just want to play, and their comments are meant as a sign that they are enjoying the game. A great performer has the skill and confidence to let them join in the game. Often the jibes and jokes of the audience can be stolen and put into the performer's act the very next show. Most of my favorite lines at one time or another either came directly from the audience or were suggested by something that was said. You don't need to be very clever on your feet to respond to these interruptions and keep hold of your end of the rope. Often, just reacting to what is being said in an honest but large way is all that is needed. Laugh if it is funny, act hurt or indignant in a mock way or even get playfully angry. You may even agree with the remark, "You think the music sounds bad from there, you should hear it from where I'm sitting."

Keep your reactions friendly and confident. Just respond in character, or let the interruption temporarily break your character. When you feel that you have properly acknowledged the interjection, go back into the character with enthusiasm and keep the game going. Remember, you are the big dog. You have control and the attention of the rest of the group. The real heckler is the one who wants to stop the game, grab the rope and walk away feeling like a winner. This kind of competitive heckler is sometimes a problem. I learned an important lesson about hecklers once while performing at Tombstone Junction in Kentucky. It was a gunfight, old train, western theme park, and I did magic in the saloon show. My friends Mac King and Lance

Burton also got their starts in magic a few years later at the same park. A white-haired, little old lady was sitting in the front row. She heckled me. I came back at her with a stock Orben line. She turned it around and beat me. A few minutes later she hit me again, and again I tried to stomp her into the ground. She was very clever, and came back with a retort much funnier than mine. This went on throughout the show, and the audience loved her. They sided with her, and I could feel the show slipping inexorably through my fingers like sand. I left the stage at the end of the show feeling beaten and robbed. Mugged by a cue-tip. I was ready to give up show business— more dejected than ever before in my life. Outgunned at the OK corral by a grandma from some little town in Kentucky. A few minutes later, I heard a knock on the dressing room door. It was the little old lady. She said, "You know son, I'm sorry if I took things too far. I just was having so much fun. You are very funny and charming, and you reminded me so much of my late husband. You know, he and I had a comedy act in Vaudeville for many years, and I was just kind of playing with you like I used to do with him. Anyway, I loved your show..."

I could have kissed her. But I learned something important. By responding to a heckler with both barrels, you become engaged in a battle of wits. It can go either way, and you never know whom you are dealing with. It could be Robin Williams out there. So, sometimes it may be better to just roll with the punch. React to the assault in a friendly way, without giving anything back that can be turned around on you. Laugh, stiffen, smile or what ever, and then give the rope a pull and go right back into the routine.

If an abusive, competitive heckler keeps attacking, wait as long as possible before firing back. This gives the audience a chance to decide that the heckler is a spoiler and come over to your side. It also gives the performer more of a chance to size up the heckler. Is he quick-witted or slow, drunk or sober? Once you sense you have the crowd with you—then you cream the bastard. The street performer must engage his crowd and win them to his cause. For that is what he is up to. He is not there to impress or to be admired. He is there to be paid. He wants the crowd to get behind him and think he's worked hard and he's very clever and look how these people are all enjoying themselves.

Several individuals in the crowd should be thinking, "Damn, I bet these jerks won't even have the decency to pay him what he deserves. I bet they don't even realize how good he is… Why, I think he's great! I'll start 'em going. Here's a buck…Come on you guys give it up!" That's what it means to get the audience enthused. You have to turn their attention and enjoyment into enthusiasm, and then turn that enthusiasm into something else. You have to enlist them in your cause. Make them want to give the performer what he is working so hard to achieve. Whether it's money, or a standing ovation, or simply taking a brochure from the company he represents, the performer must signal the audience what he wants from them, and get them on his side so that they try to encourage the others to "Hey, help the guy out…" You need to know what you want from the audience. But you also need to know what you want to give them.

Many performers have no idea why they have stepped out onto the stage. The audience then assumes that they are there to try to win their approval by impressing them. Sometimes that is all that the performer has in mind. This is the worst possible performing situation. The audience then will sit back and become critics. If the performer turns out to be the "best magician they have ever seen," they will grudgingly give him applause. If they don't like him, they will crucify him.

Almost any other goal the performer chooses is better than that. But you have to know what you are shooting for to begin with. You must know what you want **from** the audience, and you need to know what you want to **give** to them. If the performer decides he wants to scare the heck out of a crowd, and manages to do that, then they will think, "Wow, that was scary." They will applaud because they feel the performer gave them something—a good scare.

If the performer decides he wants to go out and play with the crowd, to tease them and make them laugh—to pull their legs, and he accomplishes that, then they will respond enthusiastically again. The performer can choose to make the spectators cry, to share with them his love of puns, to give them an experience of "magic," or many other goals, and all of these are better than going out without a clue what the exchange is going to be. Why are you out on the stage performing anyway? What is it that you wish to give these people, and what do you want in return? Great performers know what they want to give the audience. The street performer knows instinctively the one thing that every performer should try to figure out before going in front of a group—what he wants **from** the audience. His crowd knows what is wanted from them, and if they feel he has given them something worthwhile they will give it up. The hat will be filled.

The street performer knows exactly why he is out there in front of the crowd. Folding stuff preferred.

Footnotes

1 Taken from the Henry Ridgely Evans introduction to Tom Osborne's wonderful booklet **Cups and Balls Magic**.

2 From John Mulholland's article *The Oldest Trick*, ibid.

3 David Acer: *Confessions of a Road Warrior*, **Genii Magazine**. September, 2001.

Whit Haydn BIO

Whit Haydn works on some of the world's largest and most prestigious cruise ships, including the **QE2**, the **Norway**, and the **Westerdam**. He has performed as an opening act for Jerry Seinfeld, Loretta Lynn and many others.

Whit works for major corporations in trade shows, hospitality suites, and company banquets. The *Magic Castle* has named Whit Haydn both *Stage Magician of the Year* and *Parlor Magician of the Year*. For thirteen years the members of the **Magic Castle** have named Whit Haydn among their top five favorite close-up performers.

Whit was the chief magical consultant for the movie *Bogus* starring Whoopie Goldberg and Haley Joel Osment.

He has worked as a consultant for the film, *Houdini-They Came to See Him Die*, and for a 30 part documentary for **Canadian Discovery Channel—*Grand Illusions***. You will see him on the PAX special *Masters of Illusion*. Whit has performed at both **Caesars Palace** and **Caesars Tahoe**.

MIKAZUKI PUBLISHING HOUSE TITLES

Adventures of Jasper

Arctic Black Gold

The Bribe Vibe

Find the Ideal Husband

Learning Magic

Mikazuki Jujitsu Manual

Magic as Science & Religion

Karate 360

25 Principles of Martial Arts

Letting the Customers Win

Political Advertising Manual

Street Food War

Living the Pirate Code

Small Arms & Deep Pockets

World War Water

More Titles Coming Soon

Visit www.MikazukiPublishingHouse.com for more information on our books.

Mikazuki Publishing House is a book publishing house specializing in a variety of fiction, non-fiction, and Childrens books.

Press Contacts interested in arranging press interviews and/or author appearances, are welcome to contact:

pr@MikazukiPublishingHouse.com

We believe that the written word is the most

effective vehicle for the delivery of knowledge and

that reading is essential to educating oneself.

Mikazuki Publishing House believes in the

promotion of reading as a tool for self

progression and therefore invests resources,

working with libraries and institutions of higher

learning, to propagate the advantages of reading.

Mikazuki Publishing House is honored to be an

active participant in the fight to reverse world

deforestation.

Approximately 30 million trees are cut down in

the U.S. every year to be used for the creation of print

books. We wish to offset and counterbalance the use

of paper in the book publishing industry by working

with organizations dedicated to reversing the trend of

world deforestation. We will first start with one tree.

The consequences of not doing so could be

disastrous for future generations.

Every minute, over 160 acres of land feel the

destructive effects of deforestation. Deforestation

causes species to become extinct, disrupts

natural habitats, and erodes the top soil of viable farming lands causing drought and famine.

As a responsible book publisher, Mikazuki Publishing House will donate a percentage from the sale of each book to the effort of planting millions of trees.

Mikazuki Publishing House is pleased to invite foundations, associations, and groups dedicated to planting trees to contact us.

Please send all requests to:

philanthropy@MikazukiPublishingHouse.com

Mikazuki Publishing House enables greater exchange of knowledge by providing our authors to public institutions as guest speakers.

As our authors have limited time due to writing and book tours, we ask that you submit a request outlining the type of event with its pertinent information included.

We invite requests from the following types of organizations:

Public Libraries/Book Fairs

Event Management organizations

Community Centers

Community Colleges/Universities

Book Clubs with over 50 Active members

Please send all requests to:

philanthropy@MikazukiPublishingHouse.com

Mikazuki Publishing House is a proud member of the Independent Book Publishers Association

"EDUCATION IS THE KEY TO HAPPINESS"
KAMBIZ MOSTOFIZADEH

Printed in Great Britain
by Amazon.co.uk, Ltd.,
Marston Gate.